BinaryCoder X

Money Making Apps In 2024

"Dedicated to the digital pioneers, the seekers of financial freedom in the palm of their hand. May the exploration of 'Money Making Apps in 2024' be your compass on the path to prosperity. Here's to the dreamers who turn pixels into earnings and redefine the possibilities of a digital tomorrow."

BinaryCoder X

"Unlock the vault of digital prosperity. In the realm of Money Making Apps in 2024, BinaryCoder X is your guide to turning taps and clicks into a symphony of income. Welcome to a future where your smartphone is not just a device; it's a catalyst for financial liberation."

BinaryCoder X

Contents

1.

2.

3.

4.

5.

6.

7.

8.

9.

10.

11.

12.

13.

14.

15.

16.

17.

18.

19.

20.

21.

22.

Foreword

Foreword:

In the labyrinth of apps and algorithms, where the digital tapestry weaves opportunities in unseen patterns, BinaryCoder X stands as a beacon, guiding you through the dynamic universe of "Money Making Apps in 2024." As we stand on the precipice of a new era, BinaryCoder X extends a warm welcome to both seasoned navigators and curious beginners alike. This foreword serves as an introduction to a journey that transcends the conventional notions of income generation in the digital realm.

BinaryCoder X is not just a name; it's a testament to the prowess of deciphering the intricate codes that shape our online experiences. In this compendium, the pages are not just filled with app recommendations; they echo with the pulse of innovation and financial possibility. What lies within is not just a mere list but a curated selection of avenues that beckon you to redefine your relationship with your smartphone - turning it into a conduit for prosperity.

As you embark on this exploration, guided by the wisdom of BinaryCoder X, you'll discover that the apps listed are not merely tools but gateways to empowerment. From Swagbucks to Investing Apps, each recommendation is a carefully chosen piece in the puzzle of financial independence.

This foreword extends gratitude to BinaryCoder X for shedding light on the nexus where technology and prosperity intersect. It's an invitation to read beyond the lines and embrace the unfolding narrative of financial liberation. The journey awaits, and BinaryCoder X invites you to step into the future where your smartphone isn't just a device; it's a key to unlocking new realms of financial potential. May your journey through the pages ahead be both enlightening and enriching.

Preface

In the ever-evolving landscape of digital opportunities, the pursuit of financial empowerment takes on new dimensions. As we step into the promising realms of 2024, BinaryCoder X invites you on a captivating journey through the virtual marketplace of "Money Making Apps in 2024." In this dynamic era, where the smartphone in your hand can be a gateway to supplemental income, BinaryCoder X serves as your guide through the myriad apps designed to turn your time and skills into tangible rewards.

This exploration goes beyond the conventional, offering insights into cutting-edge applications that align with the pulse of the times. BinaryCoder X, a name synonymous with decoding digital landscapes, has curated a list that transcends the ordinary, revealing opportunities that blend seamlessly with the rhythms of modern life.

As we delve into the realms of Swagbucks, Ibotta, and beyond, this guide is not just a collection of apps but a roadmap to unlocking the potential within your digital device. Whether you're looking to earn through surveys, tap into the power of cashback, or venture into the gig economy, BinaryCoder X unveils the pathways to financial enrichment.

The pages ahead are a testament to the ever-expanding horizons of digital possibilities. With each app recommendation, BinaryCoder X illuminates the way, providing not just a list but a strategic approach to navigating the landscape of money-making apps. This preface is your invitation to embark on a journey where your smartphone becomes a tool for financial empowerment, guided by the insightful expertise of BinaryCoder X. Let the exploration begin, as we redefine the meaning of earning in the digital age.

Acknowledgement

Acknowledgment:

In the intricate dance of digital possibilities and financial landscapes, the creation of "Money Making Apps in 2024" has been a journey fueled by collaboration, expertise, and a relentless pursuit of unlocking potential. As BinaryCoder X, the architect of this exploration, stands at the forefront, it is only fitting to express profound gratitude to those who have contributed to the conception and realization of this guide.

To the tireless developers and innovators behind each money-making app featured within these pages, your commitment to pushing the boundaries of what is possible in the digital realm has not gone unnoticed. Your creations serve as the building blocks for a new narrative of financial empowerment.

To the users and enthusiasts who have shared their experiences and insights, your engagement has been invaluable. Your feedback has added depth to the understanding of how these apps resonate with diverse aspirations, making this guide richer and more meaningful.

A special acknowledgment goes to the team at BinaryCoder X, whose dedication, research, and discernment have been instrumental in curating a list that goes beyond mere recommendations. It reflects a commitment to empowering individuals in their pursuit of financial prosperity through the digital avenues available at their fingertips.

Last but not least, gratitude to the readers who embark on this journey. Your curiosity and pursuit of knowledge fuel the spirit of exploration. May the insights within these pages pave the way for new possibilities and redefine the concept of earning in the digital age.

This guide is a collective effort, a symphony of ideas, and a testament to the collaborative spirit that drives innovation. As we acknowledge each contributor, we recognize that this exploration is not merely about apps; it is about reshaping the narrative of financial independence and embracing the opportunities that the digital landscape has to offer.

With sincere thanks,

BinaryCoder   X

1

Swagbucks

To use Swagbucks:

1. Sign Up: Create an account on the Swagbucks website or app.

2. Explore Offers:Browse through surveys, watch videos, and discover various earning opportunities.

3. Complete Tasks: Take surveys, watch videos, shop online, or use Swagbucks as your search engine.

4. Earn Swagbucks (SB): Accumulate points (SB) for completing tasks.

5. Redeem Rewards: Exchange your SB for gift cards, PayPal cash, or other rewards available in the Swagbucks reward store.

Remember, consistency in completing tasks will help you accumulate more points and maximize your earnings.

2

Ibotta

To use Ibotta:

1. Download and Sign Up: Get the Ibotta app, and sign up for an account.

2. Browse Offers: Explore cashback offers on groceries, household items, and more.

3.Unlock Offers: Complete simple tasks like watching a video or answering a question to unlock cashback offers.

4. Shop: Purchase the featured items at any participating store.

5. Verify Purchases: Take a photo of your receipt within the app to verify your purchases.

6. Get Cashback: Earn cashback, which can be transferred to your PayPal account or redeemed for gift cards.

Using Ibotta is a straightforward way to save money on everyday purchases by earning cashback on eligible items.

3

Survey Junkie

To use Survey Junkie:

1. Sign Up: Create an account on the Survey Junkie platform.

2. Complete Profile: Fill out your profile to receive surveys tailored to your demographics.

3. Browse Available Surveys: Explore the list of available surveys and their corresponding rewards.

4. Take Surveys: Participate in surveys by answering questions and providing your opinions.

5. Earn Points: Accumulate points for each completed survey.

6. Redeem Rewards: Exchange your points for cash through PayPal or e-gift cards.

Consistency in participating in surveys and keeping your profile updated can enhance your opportunities to receive more relevant survey invitations.

4

Acorns

To use Acorns:

1. Download and Sign Up: Install the Acorns app and create an account.

2. Connect Your Accounts: Link your debit/credit cards and bank accounts to Acorns.

3. Round-Up Purchases: Enable the round-up feature to invest spare change from everyday purchases.

4. Choose Investment Portfolio: Select an investment portfolio based on your risk tolerance and financial goals.

5. Automate Contributions: Set up automatic contributions to grow your investment over time.

6. Monitor and Adjust: Keep track of your investment performance and make adjustments as needed.

Acorns offers a user-friendly way to start investing with small amounts, making it accessible for individuals looking to grow their savings effortlessly.

5

Rakuten

To use Rakuten:

1. Sign Up: Create an account on the Rakuten website or app.

2. Browse Stores: Explore the list of partner stores offering cashback deals.

3. Activate Cashback: Click on a store through Rakuten before making a purchase to activate cashback.

4. Shop as Usual: Make your purchase on the store's website as you normally would.

5. Earn Cashback: Rakuten will track your purchase and reward you with cashback.

6. Receive Payouts: Receive your accumulated cashback through PayPal or a check.

Rakuten makes it easy to earn cashback on your online purchases by simply going through their platform before making a purchase.

6

TaskRabbit

To use TaskRabbit:

1. Sign Up: Create an account on the TaskRabbit website or app.

2. Set Your Skills: Specify the tasks you're skilled at and willing to perform.

3. Browse Tasks: Explore available tasks in your local area.

4. Submit Bids: Submit bids for tasks you're interested in, including your proposed rate.

5. Get Hired: If the task poster accepts your bid, coordinate details and complete the task.

6. Get Paid: Receive payment through the TaskRabbit platform once the task is completed.

TaskRabbit connects you with local tasks that match your skills, providing a flexible way to earn money by helping others with various tasks.

7

Uber or Lyft

To use Uber or Lyft:

1. Download the App:Install the Uber or Lyft app on your smartphone.

2. Create an Account: Sign up and provide necessary information, including a valid payment method.

3. Verify Identity: Complete any required identity verification steps.

4. Set Your Availability: Indicate when you're available to drive.

5. Accept Rides: When you're ready, start accepting ride requests through the app.

6. Complete Trips: Drive passengers to their destinations safely and efficiently.

7. Get Paid: Earn money based on the number of completed trips, with payment processed through the app.

Uber and Lyft provide a flexible way to earn income by offering transportation services in your own vehicle.

8

Fiverr

T o use Fiverr:

1. Sign Up:Create a Fiverr account on their website or app.

2. Create a Gig: Define the service you're offering and set a price for it.

3. Build Your Profile: Showcase your skills and experience on your Fiverr profile.

4. Publish Your Gig: Make your service (Gig) live on the platform.

5. Promote Your Services: Share your Fiverr profile on social media and other platforms.

6. Receive Orders: Users interested in your service will place orders.

7. Deliver Work: Complete the orders according to the agreed-upon terms.

8. Get Paid: Fiverr will handle the payment, and you'll receive your earnings through the platform.

Fiverr is a popular freelance platform where you can offer a wide range of services, from writing and graphic design to programming and marketing.

9

Foap

To use Foap:

1. Download the App: Install the Foap app on your smartphone.

2. Create an Account: Sign up and set up your profile.

3. Upload Photos: Upload high-quality photos from your gallery to the Foap marketplace.

4. Tag and Describe: Add relevant tags and descriptions to your photos to enhance discoverability.

5. Submit to Missions: Participate in Foap missions to earn additional rewards.

6. Wait for Sales: Your photos are available for purchase by individuals and businesses.

7. Get Paid: Earn money when someone buys the rights to use your photo.

Foap provides a platform for photographers to monetize their images by selling them to a wide audience.

10

Upwork

To use Upwork:

1. Create a Profile: Sign up on the Upwork website and create a detailed freelancer profile.

2. Define Your Skills: Clearly specify your skills, experience, and expertise.

3. Set Your Rates: Determine your hourly or project-based rates.

4. Search for Jobs: Browse through available job postings and submit proposals for projects.

5. Complete Skills Tests: Take relevant skills tests to enhance your profile.

6. Communicate with Clients: Discuss project details with potential clients through the platform.

7. Deliver Quality Work: If hired, complete the assigned tasks or projects to the best of your ability.

8. Get Paid: Receive payments securely through the Upwork platform.

Upwork is a freelancing platform that connects freelancers with clients seeking various skills, making it a versatile platform for remote work opportunities.

11

Decluttr

To use Decluttr:

1. Download the App or Visit Website: Access Decluttr through their website or app.

2.Scan Items: Use the app to scan barcodes of CDs, DVDs, tech gadgets, and other items you want to sell.

3. Get Valuations: Receive instant valuations for your scanned items.

4. Add to Basket: Add accepted items to your basket.

5. Complete Transaction: Provide necessary information and complete the transaction.

6. Ship Items: Decluttr will provide a free shipping label for you to send your items.

7. Get Paid: Once your items are received and verified, you'll receive payment through your chosen method.

Decluttr simplifies the process of selling unwanted items, turning clutter into cash.

12

Airbnb

To host experiences on Airbnb:

1. Create an Airbnb Account: Sign up on Airbnb and complete your profile.

2. Navigate to "Host": Access the hosting section on the platform.

3. List Your Experience: Provide details about the experience you want to host, including a description, duration, and any requirements.

4. Set the Price: Determine the cost for participants to join your experience.

5. Add Photos: Include high-quality photos that showcase what participants can expect.

6. Availability: Set your availability schedule for the experience.

7. Publish Your Experience: Once everything is set up, publish your experience on Airbnb.

8. Communicate with Participants: Respond to inquiries, coordinate meeting points, and provide any necessary details.

9. Host the Experience: Ensure a great experience for participants.

10. Receive Payments: Airbnb handles the payment process, and you'll receive your earnings through the platform.

Airbnb Experiences allow you to share your passions and skills with travelers, providing unique and authentic experiences in your local area.

13

UserTesting

To use UserTesting:

1. Sign Up: Create an account on the UserTesting platform.

2. Complete Your Profile: Provide demographic information to match with relevant testing opportunities.

3. Take a Practice Test: Familiarize yourself with the testing process by completing a practice test.

4. Wait for Test Invitations: UserTesting will notify you when there are available tests matching your profile.

5. Take Tests: Follow instructions to navigate websites or apps while sharing your thoughts via audio and video.

6. Submit Feedback: Provide honest feedback about your experience during the test.

7. Get Paid: Receive compensation for each completed test via PayPal.

UserTesting offers a simple way to earn money by sharing your user experience insights with companies looking to improve their websites and apps.

14

Dosh

To use Dosh:

1. Download and Sign Up: Install the Dosh app on your smartphone and create an account.

2. Link Your Cards: Connect your credit or debit cards securely to the Dosh app.

3. Browse Offers: Explore cashback deals available at participating retailers and restaurants.

4. Shop as Usual: Make purchases using linked cards at Dosh-affiliated businesses.

5. Earn Cashback: Automatically earn cashback, which is credited to your Dosh account.

6.Cash Out: Once you reach a minimum threshold, transfer your earnings to your bank account or PayPal.

Dosh simplifies the cashback process by automatically crediting your account when you make qualifying purchases at supported merchants.

15

Field Agent:

T o use Field Agent:

1. Download the App: Install the Field Agent app on your smartphone.

2. Create an Account: Sign up and complete your profile.

3. Find Available Tasks: Browse the list of available tasks in your local area.

4. Accept a Task: Select a task that interests you and fits your schedule.

5. Complete the Task: Follow the instructions for the task and provide the required information.

6. Submit Results: Upload any necessary photos or details as instructed for task completion.

7. Get Paid: Receive payment for the completed task through the Field Agent app.

Field Agent allows you to earn money by completing short tasks, such as checking product displays or gathering information, in your local area.

16

Poshmark

To use Poshmark:

1. Download the App: Install the Poshmark app on your smartphone.

2. Create an Account: Sign up and set up your seller profile.

3. List Your Items: Take quality photos of your clothing and accessories, and create listings.

4. Set Prices: Determine the selling prices for your items.

5. Share Listings: Promote your listings by sharing them with the Poshmark community.

6. Communicate with Buyers: Respond to inquiries, negotiate prices, and provide additional information.

7. Ship Items: Once sold, package and ship the items to buyers.

8. Receive Payments: Poshmark handles the transaction, and you receive earnings once the buyer confirms receipt.

Poshmark is a platform where you can sell secondhand clothing and accessories, creating a virtual closet for buyers to browse and purchase from.

17

Teachable

To use Teachable:

1. Sign Up: Create an account on the Teachable platform.

2. Set Up Your School: Build your online school by adding a logo, choosing a domain, and customizing the look.

3. Create a Course: Develop your course content using Teachable's tools for text, video, quizzes, and more.

4. Set Pricing: Decide whether your course will be free or paid, and set the price accordingly.

5. Market Your Course: Promote your course through social media, email, or other channels.

6. Enroll Students: Learners can sign up and enroll in your course.

7. Deliver Content: Students access course materials, and you can interact with them through the platform.

8. Receive Payments: Teachable manages payments, and you receive earnings according to your pricing structure.

Teachable is a platform that enables you to create and sell online courses, making it accessible for individuals looking to share their expertise and earn money through education.

18

42

Chegg Tutors

To use Chegg Tutors:

1. Sign Up: Create an account on the Chegg Tutors platform.

2. Complete Your Profile: Provide information about your expertise, qualifications, and subjects you can teach.

3. Set Availability: Indicate when you're available for tutoring sessions.

4. Apply for Subjects: Apply to become a tutor for specific subjects you excel in.

5. Get Matched with Students: Chegg will match you with students seeking tutoring in your areas of expertise.

6. Schedule Sessions: Coordinate with students to schedule tutoring sessions.

7. Conduct Sessions: Provide tutoring services through the online platform.

8. Get Paid: Chegg handles payments, and you receive compensation for your tutoring sessions.

Chegg Tutors is an online platform that connects students with tutors for various subjects, offering a flexible way to share your knowledge and earn income.

19

Amazon Mechanical Turk

To use Amazon Mechanical Turk:

1. Sign Up: Create an account on the Amazon Mechanical Turk (MTurk) platform.

2. Complete Your Profile: Fill out your profile with accurate information.

3. Browse Tasks (HITs): Explore the available Human Intelligence Tasks (HITs) on the platform.

4. Accept and Complete Tasks: Choose tasks that interest you, accept them, and complete as instructed.

5. Submit Work: After completing a task, submit your work according to the guidelines provided.

6. Get Paid: Receive payment for approved tasks; payments are often small and can accumulate over time.

MTurk offers a marketplace for individuals and businesses to crowdsource small tasks, providing a way for users to earn money by completing these micro-tasks.

20

Robinhood

To use Investing Apps (e.g., Robinhood):

1. Download the App: Install the investing app, such as Robinhood, on your smartphone.

2. Create an Account: Sign up and complete the account setup process.

3. Link Your Bank Account: Connect your bank account to fund your investment activities.

4. Explore Investments: Browse and research stocks, ETFs, or other investment options available on the platform.

5. Make Investments: Purchase shares of stocks or other assets based on your investment strategy.

6. Monitor Your Portfolio: Keep track of your investments and their performance through the app.

7. Stay Informed: Stay updated on market news and trends to make informed investment decisions.

8. Withdraw or Reinvest: Depending on your goals, you can withdraw profits or reinvest earnings to further grow your portfolio.

Investing apps provide a user-friendly way to enter the stock market and other financial markets, making it accessible for individuals to start building their investment portfolios.